First World War
and Army of Occupation
War Diary
France, Belgium and Germany

16 DIVISION
48 Infantry Brigade
Royal Munster Fusiliers
2nd Battalion
1 February 1918 - 31 May 1918

WO95/1975/4

The Naval & Military Press Ltd
www.nmarchive.com
Published in association with The National Archives

Published by

The Naval & Military Press Ltd

Unit 10 Ridgewood Industrial Park,

Uckfield, East Sussex,

TN22 5QE England

Tel: +44 (0) 1825 749494

www.naval-military-press.com

www.nmarchive.com

This diary has been reprinted in facsimile from the original. Any imperfections are inevitably reproduced and the quality may fall short of modern type and cartographic standards.

© **Crown Copyright**
Images reproduced by permission of The National Archives, London, England, 2015.

Contents

Document type	Place/Title	Date From	Date To
Heading	1975/4 1918 Feb-May 2 Battalion Royal Munster Fusiliers		
Heading	16th Division 48th Infy Bde 2nd Bn Roy. Munster Fus Feb-May 1918 From 1 Div. 3 Bde To 50 Div 150 Bde		
Heading	2nd R. Munster Fus Feb 1918		
Heading	War Diary for Month of February, 1918 Unit:- 2nd Ro. Munster Fusrs.		
War Diary	Camp G A16a62	01/02/1918	02/02/1918
War Diary	Longavesnes Farm Sheet 62c E25bd	03/02/1918	06/02/1918
War Diary	Longavesnes Ref. Map France Sheet 62.c	06/02/1918	06/02/1918
War Diary	Near St Emelie E.24.a	07/02/1918	11/02/1918
War Diary	Grafton Post to Mule Lane	11/02/1918	11/02/1918
War Diary	Trenches as above	12/02/1918	16/02/1918
War Diary	Ref map Lempire 1/10000 Trenches Grafton Post to Mule Lane F.5.c.7.a to f.4.a.6.6	17/02/1918	18/02/1918
War Diary	Support Billet round Lempire F.15a.90.35	19/02/1918	19/02/1918
War Diary	Support Billets F15 A 90 35 Ref Map Lempire 1/10000	20/02/1918	22/02/1918
War Diary	Trenches X26 and F.2x3	23/02/1918	23/02/1918
War Diary	Trenches x26 & F2 & 3 Ref Map Lempire 1/10000	24/02/1918	28/04/1918
Operation(al) Order(s)	2nd Battalion The Royal Munster Fusiliers Operation Orders No. 7	31/01/1918	31/01/1918
Miscellaneous	2nd Battalion The Royal Munster Fusiliers.		
Operation(al) Order(s)	2nd. Battn. The Royal Munster Fusiliers. Operation Order No. 8	01/02/1918	01/02/1918
Miscellaneous	Report Of Attempted Raid At F.5.c.5.4. Refce Map Lempire 1/10000: Night 11th-12th February 1918	12/02/1918	12/02/1918
Miscellaneous	48th Infantry Brigade. No. G.59/4	12/02/1918	12/02/1918
Operation(al) Order(s)	2nd Battalion The Royal Munster Fusiliers "Operation Order. No. 9"	05/02/1918	05/02/1918
Operation(al) Order(s)	2nd Battalion The Royal Munster Fusiliers "Operation Order. No. 10"		
Operation(al) Order(s)	2nd Battn The Royal Munster Fusiliers. Operation Order. No. 12	22/02/1918	22/02/1918
Operation(al) Order(s)	2nd Battn. The Royal Munster Fusiliers Operation Order. No. 11	17/02/1918	17/02/1918
Heading	48th Brigade 16th Division. Diary 1st to 20th March 1918 missing 2nd Battalion The Royal Munster Fusiliers March 1918 Appendices attached Report from captured officer of the regiment		
Miscellaneous	2nd Battn The Roy. Munster Fusiliers.	06/04/1918	06/04/1918
Miscellaneous	1a/49833.C. (40963) Holzminden	13/04/1918	13/04/1918
Heading	2nd R Munster Fus April 1918		
Heading	War Diary of 2nd R. Munster Fus for Month of April 1918		
War Diary	Amiens Map Hamel	01/04/1918	03/04/1918
War Diary	Amiens Map Dieppe Map	03/04/1918	04/04/1918
War Diary	Rambures	05/04/1918	08/04/1918
War Diary	Ref Maps Dieppe Abbeville	09/04/1918	09/04/1918
War Diary	Ref Map Abbeville Hazebrouck	10/04/1918	11/04/1918
War Diary	Happe	12/04/1918	13/04/1918

War Diary	Ref Map Hazebrouck 5a Calais B	13/04/1918	14/04/1918
War Diary	Hazebrouck 5a Map	14/04/1918	15/04/1918
War Diary	Steenbecque	16/04/1918	16/04/1918
War Diary	Hazebrouck 5a-Map Steenbecque	16/04/1918	21/04/1918
War Diary	Hazebrouck 5a Map	22/04/1918	22/04/1918
War Diary	Wavrans	23/04/1918	25/04/1918
War Diary	Hazebrouck 5a Map Wavrans	25/04/1918	29/04/1918
War Diary	Hazebrouck 5a Map Vaudringhem	29/04/1918	30/04/1918
Miscellaneous	48th Infantry Brigade. 2nd Bn Royal Munster Fusiliers. Appendix A	21/03/1918	21/03/1918
Miscellaneous	Battalion Orders By Lieut-Col. H.B. Tonson-Rye. Commanding. 2nd Battalion The Royal Munster Fusiliers in The Field.	22/04/1918	22/04/1918
Heading	2nd R. Munster Fus May 1918		
War Diary	Ref Map Hazebrouck Vaudringhem	01/05/1918	13/05/1918
War Diary	Ref Map Calais Dignopre	14/05/1918	15/05/1918
War Diary	Desvres	16/05/1918	16/05/1918
War Diary	Ref Map Calais Desvres	17/05/1918	19/05/1918
War Diary	Hesdin L'Abbe	20/05/1918	20/05/1918
War Diary	Ref Map Calais Hesdin L'Abbe	20/05/1918	30/05/1918
War Diary	Racquinghem	31/05/1918	31/05/1918
Miscellaneous	2nd Battalion The Royal Gun Fusiliers.	04/05/1918	04/05/1918
Miscellaneous	2nd Battalion The Royal Munster Fusiliers. Training Programme For Week Ending Saturday, 18th May 1918.35	18/05/1918	18/05/1918
Miscellaneous	2nd Battalion The Royal Munster Fusiliers. Training Programme Of Above Unit For Week Ending	25/05/1918	25/05/1918
Miscellaneous	2nd Bn The Royal Munster Fusiliers "Training Programme For Week Ending Saturday 11th May, 1918	11/05/1918	11/05/1918

19 75/4
1915 feb - may
2 Battalion Royal Munster Fusiliers

16TH DIVISION
48TH INFY BDE

2ND BN ROY. MUNSTER FUS.

FEB - MAY 1918

From 1 DIV. 3 BDE
To 50 DIV 150 BDE

2nd R. Munster fus

FEB 1918

WAR DIARY.

FOR MONTH OF FEBRUARY, 1918.

VOLUME:-

UNIT:- 2nd. Bn. Munster Fusrs.

Army Form C. 2118.

WAR DIARY
or
INTELLIGENCE SUMMARY. SECRET.
(Erase heading not required.)

Instructions regarding War Diaries and Intelligence Summaries are contained in F. S. Regs., Part II. and the Staff Manual respectively. Title pages will be prepared in manuscript.

Place	Date Feby	Hour	Summary of Events and Information	Remarks and references to Appendices
CAMP 6 A16A82	1st		The Battalion handed Filt Operation Order No 7 dated 31/1/17 for CANAL BANK to Camp 6. Bond 1st Platoon Played B. first Elff of and Fifteen 1st Plat Wheel band. Elff. Gpain Base Bags S.W. Fifthringh O.C. Transferred to 1st Bⁿ (Lt P.T. PENANT to leave U.K.) Revᵈ F.A. GLEESON C.F. Att⁴ Bⁿ proceeded to re attached to Bⁿ	Operation Order No 7 - 31/1/17 attached
"	2nd		The Battalion handed to Operation Order No 8 dated 1/2/15 and entrained for TINCOURT BOUCLY; then debating S Johan	Operation Order No 8 - 1/2/15 attached
LONGAVESNES Cump Hut- G.16 E25A4	3rd		Arrived T. BOUCLY 9.3 am; debussed & marched to LONGAVESNES. Magᵗ General L. W. Hickey, Ontg 16ᵗ(Irish) Divᶻⁿ in and Lt. Col. Wolf, Pt. Q.M.G.R.S. invited Bⁿ then at Stu. Buffalo Talks to 4 B" of f. Plo Mostly of interest Battalion took in enemy	
"	4ᵗʰ		" Report of Officers & N.C.O; recomtal Vanna	
"	5ᵗʰ		"	
"	6ᵗʰ		B: Instruction & offensive field strips	

Army Form C. 2118.

WAR DIARY
or
INTELLIGENCE SUMMARY. SECRET
(Erase heading not required.)

Instructions regarding War Diaries and Intelligence Summaries are contained in F. S. Regs., Part II. and the Staff Manual respectively. Title pages will be prepared in manuscript.

Place	Date	Hour	Summary of Events and Information	Remarks and references to Appendices
LONE AVESNES [Ref March] 62.C.	February 1918 6		Battalion marched try and went Reserve Area E.24.a. where they were accommodated in dug outs or sitting on light railway near STEENWERCK	Operation order No.9 - 5/2/18 attached (marked)
FRANCE Sheet 62.C.			Battalion in reserve to 48 INF BDE holding the line from (Ref Map) LEMPIRE 1/10000 F.11.a - 6.6. to X.26.d.9.3.	
near STEENWERCK E.24.a	7		Battalion as above furnishing working parties up to 200 ORanks. Relief from 3" reconciled 10 Feb A/L Major R R S KANE D.S.O transferred to 1st Bn R MUNSTER FUS to Command	
	8		Battalion as above furnishing working parties. 66 O.R. to B.D.E. and Div. Employment.	
	9		Battalion as above furnishing working parties. LT J.P.F.FLOOD R.A.M.C. to Hospital LT T MCELNEA to leave U.K. LT J.B. MINFORD R.A.M.C. joined the Batta	

WAR DIARY or INTELLIGENCE SUMMARY

Army Form C. 2118.

Place	Date	Hour	Summary of Events and Information	Remarks and references to Appendices
Near ST EMELIE	February 1917 10 (Sunday)		Battalion on station. Battalion moved into the line by sub-units arrived at 6 a.m. relieving 2" R. DUBLIN FUSILIERS in the trenches. The battalion left the Camp camp LEMPIRE 1000 to from F.5.c.70 to F.6.a.6.6. A Coy in right in GRAFTON POST. "C" Coy in centre at HEYTHROP and "B" Coy in left in MULE TRENCH. "D" Coy in support at SANDBAG ALLEY, YAK and ZEBRA POSTS Bn H.Q. F.10.c.4.5. The 17" 47 INF Bde on right holding TOMBOIS POST and the 1" R. DUBLIN FUSILIERS on left holding continuation of MULE TRENCH. Strength 3 Offrs in trenches. Casualties nil. B" sent out 2 patrols. 23 officers 547 O. Ranks. 2 Lt R.J. MAUNSELL-EYRE joined the Bn	Operation order attached Orders attached Marches attached
TRENCHES	11"		Battalion holding the line as above. An attempt to capture a German post at F.5.c.45-35 was made by the enemy who surprised the post from the rear. They did not succeed in capturing any prisoners or material, 10 rifles etc. were captured from the enemy. Casualties 3 wounded. B" sent out 2 patrols.	
GRAFTON POST			Lt W. S. KIDD from leave - U.K.	
& MULE LANE			Regt J. FLYNN Sr. C.F. joined battalion for duty vice Rev. F. GLEESON who remained with 3 BDE	

Army Form C. 2118.

WAR DIARY SECRET
or
INTELLIGENCE SUMMARY.
(Erase heading not required.)

Instructions regarding War Diaries and Intelligence Summaries are contained in F. S. Regs., Part II. and the Staff Manual respectively. Title pages will be prepared in manuscript.

Place	Date	Hour	Summary of Events and Information	Remarks and references to Appendices
TRENCHES as above	February 12		Battalion holding line as above. Patrols sent out under 2nd Lts WELCH and CLAIR. No casualties.	
"	13		Battn holding line as above. No casualties. 2Lt J.W. GILLMAN to leave U.K. Patrolling carried out as usual.	
"	14		Battn holding line as above. 1 Casualty (wounded) Fighting patrolised out under 2LT WELCH. 2 RDF relieved 1" RDF in Battn left night 14/15 Strength Battalion Total 42 officers 821 OR's Co.Strength 34 " 652 OR's Trench 25 " 487 OR's	
"	15		Battn holding line as above. No casualties. Patrolling as usual. 2LT J.W.GILLMAN to leave U.K.	
"	16		Battn holding line as above. No casualties. Patrols as usual.	

Army Form C. 2118.

WAR DIARY SECRET
INTELLIGENCE SUMMARY.
(Erase heading not required.)

Instructions regarding War Diaries and Intelligence Summaries are contained in F.S. Regs., Part II. and the Staff Manual respectively. Title pages will be prepared in manuscript.

Place	Date	Hour	Summary of Events and Information	Remarks and references to Appendices
Rd and LEMPIRE TRENCHES	Feby 17 1918		Battalion Holding line No casualties. Fighting patrol out under 2/Lt THORNLEY which did not encounter enemy	
CRAFTON POST			CAPT R.H CRICHTON M.C. to join TANK CORPS	
KNULE LANE			CAPT R.M TREN A.S.C. attached for duty	
F.5.c.7.a. F.14.a.6.6			39 O.R's reinforcements joined Battalion	
	18th		3. Battalion Holding line as above. 1 Coy (W). Battalion was relieved in the line by the 1st R.D.F. night 18/19 and proceeded to support Alt. Bⁿ Operation Order No 11 disposed to follow:- BHQ LEMPIRE F.15.a.90.35. "A" and "C" Companies {CAPT. NEWENHAM attached (CAPT. CHANDLER M.C.} MALASSISE FARM F.2.d.0.1. and "D" & {LT KIDD} F.15.a.23	
			LT C.M.T. RYAN M.C. Transport Officer wounded whilst of duty.	
supp^t Falls 9. LEMPIRE F.15 & 20. 35.	19th		Battalion in support in strict furnishing working parties 1 about 385 all ranks has been. Bⁿ set up a fighting patrol LT McKEOWN 23 O.R's to his which went out from F.5.c.6.1 about 3 am 20 inst. Patrol encountered hostile patrol about 75 strong at about F.5.t.6.2. A combat ensued in he trans bond and enemy withdraws with their wounded some casualties. Patrol returned to our lines without casualties LT. W.T. PHILIPS to H^d sick	

WAR DIARY or INTELLIGENCE SUMMARY

Army Form C. 2118.

Place	Date	Hour	Summary of Events and Information	Remarks and references to Appendices
Support Trenches F15 a 90 35	February 1918 20th		Battalion in Support furnishing large working parties. No casualties. 1 RDF in line on right, 2 RDF on left. LT. H.O. WHELAN M.C. & team U.K.	
Reg Hd. EMPIRE Lines	21st		Battalion in support. No casualties. Large working parties.	
"	22nd		Battalion in support. No casualties. Battalion relieved 2.RDF in line on left sector at night 22/23. 1 casualty (accident?) Battalion disposed as follows. "D" and "B" Companies holding front line & support line from (attached) F.4.5.7.6. X 27 c 6.5. C H D D "C" Fds q "B" "C" F 2 & 3.8. "B" Cy in Support "A" Cy in reserve at TETARD WOOD BH a Fld 8.8. 1st Bn RDF on B. night. 49 B.De 4/7 INNIS. FUS. on B. left Relieved at the same relief. LT J.J. MURPHY to H. sick	Observation Order No 12
Trenches N.26 and F.2+3	23rd		Battalion holding the line as above. Fighting patrol out. No casualties. 2nd LT H.I. SHAPBOLT & H. sick 18 Regt S.I. Hs.	

WAR DIARY SECRET
or
INTELLIGENCE SUMMARY.
(Erase heading not required.)

Army Form C. 2118.

Place	Date	Hour	Summary of Events and Information	Remarks and references to Appendices
Trenches X.26. F.2. 3 MAYLEMPIRE / Lowe	24th		Battalion holding the line as above. Fighting patrol out. No casualties. LT. P.M. ARDAGH to hosp. V.K.	
	25th		Battalion holding line as above. Patrol out. No casualties.	
	26th		Battalion holding line as above. Patrol out. 2 LT M BOLAND killed in action at C.H.D. by a S.N.	
	27th		Battalion holding line as above. Patrol out. No casualties. 18 Regt (9th I. Horse Bn) relieved 7 Inniskillen Fus on B" left	
	28th		Battalion holding line as above. 21st Divn (8 Leicester Regt 110th Bde) relieved 7 Irish Regt on B" left. No casualties. Strength 1 Bn 28 inst.	

Strength 1 Bn 22 Officers 510 O.Ranks
C O's Strength 27 Officers 672 O.Ranks
on Command 12 — 161 O.Ranks
Total 39 — 833 O.Ranks

[signature] Lt Col
Commdg 2 R. I/3/18

"SECRET."

Copy No........1........

"2ND BATTALION THE ROYAL MUNSTER FUSILIERS."

"OPERATION ORDER No. 7." Dated 31.1.18.

Reference Map Sheet 28. 1/20,000.

(1). The Battalion will move by Route March to Camp C.-A.16.a.6.2., on the 1st February, 1918.

(2). Route :- BRIELEN - ELVERDINGHE - DROMORE CORNER - DEWIPPE CABARET.
Order of Companies :- "Hd.Quarter Coy", "D", "A", "B" and "C" Coys.
Starting Point :- Road Junction - C.25.a.3.8.
Time :- 9.45.a.m.
Dress :- Marching Order. Caps.

(3). Cookers, Water Carts and Mess Cart will march 100 yards in rear of the last Company.

(4). Blankets and Officers' Kits will be stacked N. of Cook House at 8.30 a.m.

(5). Rear Party :- Lieut. G.W.Gillman, and 12 other ranks of Sapper Platoon will remain to Police Billets and hand over to incoming Unit.

(6). The Mess Cart for Headquarters and "A" Coy will be on the road outside Hd.Quarters at 8.45.a.m.
Other Company Mess Stores will be carried on the Cookers.

Issued at...11.30...a.m.

Captain. Adjutant.
2nd Battalion The Royal Munster Fusiliers.

Copies to :-
No.1. War Diary.
 2. Office.
 3. A.Coy.
 4. B.Coy.
 5. C.Coy.
 6. D.Coy.
 7. Transport Officer.
 8. Qr.Master.
 9. R.S.M.
 10. Captain.B.H.Purdon.

2ND BATTALION THE ROYAL MUNSTER FUSILIERS.

Reference Map 28. 1/20,000.

(1). The Details at SIEGE CAMP and Battalion Transport will move on the 1st February to Camp G.(A.16.a.6.2).

(2). An advance party, Captain.B.H.Purdon,4.N.C.Os. and 12 Privates will proceed at 8.30.a.m.

(3). Remainder of Details and Battalion Transport will march at 9.15. a.m. with pr-oper intervals.

Route :- By DEWIPTE CABARET.

xxxxxxxxxxxxxxxxxxxxxxxxxxxxxxxxxxxxxxxxxxxxxxxxxxxxxxxxxxxxxxxxxxxx

In the Field.   Captain.Adjutant.

31.1.18.   2nd Battalion The Royal Munster Fusiliers.

SECRET.   Copy No. 1

2nd. Battn. The Royal Munster Fusiliers.
Operation Orders No. 8.

Reference Map Sheet 28.1/40000.

1. The Battalion will march to ESKIMOEK tomorrow, and there entrain.

2. Order of March:- Headquarters, "A", "B", "C", "D".
   Route by INTERNATIONAL CORNER.
   Starting Point. Point in the road through the Camp 200.yards EAST of Guard Room.
   Time.   2.30.p.m.
   Dress.   Marching Order. Caps will be worn.
   Intervals.   100.yards between Coys.

3. Lieut.H.J.SHADBOLT and 58 other ranks from "A"Coy. will move past starting point at 1.15.p.m. On arrival at entraining point, they will pile arms, remove equipment and entrain transport and stores.

4. Transport will move 100.yards in rear of loading party and entrain at 2.p.m.

5. Rations for 3rd.inst. will be carried by men.
   Teas will be served at entraining point at 4.p.m.

6. 2/Lieut.J.W.GILLMAN and 12.other ranks (Sapper Platoon) will hand over billets to the AREA COMMANDANT.
   Usual certificates re cleanliness of billets to be rendered by Coys.
   2.nd.in Command will go round billets with W.O. at 2.30.p.m.

7. 2/Lieut.H.J.McBLENE and C.Q.M.Sergeants with entraining strengths of their Coys.will be at entraining point at 2.p.m. They will report to the Adjutant before leaving, for orders.

8. One "G" will be the signal for men to be allowed to leave the train.
   Two "G's" all men will at once entrain.

Issued at 8.5. p.m.   C.O'Callaghan 2/Lt for Captain,
1st. February. 1918.   Adjutant, 2nd. Battn. The Royal Munster Fusiliers

Copy.NO. 1. War Diary.
   "   " 2. Office.
   "   " 3. "A"Coy.
   "   " 4. "B"Coy.
   "   " 5. "C"Coy.
   "   " 6. "D"Coy.
   "   " 7. Transport Officer.
   "   " 8. Quartermaster.

REPORT OF ATTEMPTED RAID AT F.5.c.5.4.

Refce Map LEMPIRE 1/10,000:   Night 11th - 12th February 1918

A L.G. post, which is very well known to the enemy is about 150 yds from nearest group in GRAFTON POST. Enemy apparently crossed our wire at GRAFTON TRENCH about F.11.a.7.7., advanced into our back area, and fell upon the L.G. post from the rear.

This patrol seems to have been seen by 6th CONNAUGHT RANGERS on our RIGHT, who estimated it at about 20 strong; they also, I understand, saw it leaving. They thought it was a wiring party of ours, and sent up a small patrol to us to definitely ascertain.

The enemy dropped down from the rear upon our men who were standing, 2 on sentry at the Lewis Gun, and 4 leaning against the back of the trench near by. The enemy were about 10 in number. A struggle ensued, which resulted in our men getting away with their L. Gun. They had no chance of using rifle and bayonet, owing to surprise and the narrow trench. The enemy had come provided with knives and sticks, which he freely used.

We suffered three casualties (wounded), 2 from knife thrusts, and one from apparently a revolver bullet.

Enemy retired by route of entry.

He left on the scene some caps (forwarded for identification), bombs, and a Mauser rifle. I doubt if he suffered any casualties.

(Sd) H. IRELAND, Lt-Col.,
Commanding 2nd R. Munster Fusiliers.

12-2-18

To:-   16th Division.

48th Infantry Brigade. No. G.59/4   12th Feby 1918

Reference telephone conversation.

Patrols pass from GRAFTON POST to the RIGHT Battalion post at irregular intervals during the night. This is also the case with patrols from the Battalion on their right.

One of our patrols had been down the trench and returned at about 9.0 o'clock, but had nothing to report.

A patrol from the Right Battalion arrived at our post shortly after the raid.

A.B. Thompson   Lieut-Colonel.
Commanding 48th Infantry Brigade.

"SECRET."   Copy No........1......

"2ND BATTALION THE ROYAL MUNSTER FUSILIERS."

"OPERATION   ORDER.   NO. 9...."   Dated 5.2.18.

Reference Map France. Sheet 52.c.

(1). The Battalion will move to Reserve aera= E.24.a., by Route March tomorrow.

(2). Order of March :- "Hd.Qr.Coy.", "B", "C", "D" and "A" Coys.
Starting Point :- E.25.d.7.9.
Time :- 4.15.p.m.
Interval of 200 yards will be maintained between Coys.
Dress :- Marching Order.   Caps.

(3). An advance party of 1.Officer, 3.Other Ranks per Coy. Sergt. R.O'Sullivan and 8.Other Ranks of the Sapper Platoon will proceed by Route March at 2.p.m. and take over Billets from 2nd Roy Dublin Fusiliers.
The Senior Officer will report at Battn Hd.Quarters at 1.45.p.m. for instructions.

(4). Blankets and Officers Kits will be stacked at or inside Coy Billets by 10.a.m.

(5). Rear Party. 2nd Lieut.G.W.Gillman and remainder of Sapper Platoon will arrange to hand over Billets to Area Commandant at 4.p.m. Usual Certificates will be handed in to the Adjutant from Coys. The 2nd in Command and Battn Medical Officer will inspect Billets at 4.p.m.

(6). Cookers will march in rear of Battalion to vicinity of Reserve aera.
Kettles will then be removed from them and they will return to Waggon Lines.

(7). Drums will play with "B" Coy for 20 minutes and "C" Coy for 20 min and then proceed to Waggon Lines.

(8). Details for Waggon Lines will proceed there by Route March under Lieut.C.E.A.O'Callaghan. at 3 p.m.

(9). ACKNOWLEGE.

xxxxxxxxxxxxxxxxxxxxxxxxxxxxxxxxxxxxxxxxxxxxxxxxxxxxxxxxxxxxxxxx

Issued at....... p.m.
                                                              Captain.
                    Adjutant.2nd Battalion The Royal Munster Fusiliers.

Copies to :-
No.1. War Diary.
   2. Office.
   3. A.Coy.
   4. B.Coy.
   5. C.Coy.
   6. D.Coy.
   7. Transport Officer.
   8. QR.Master.
   9. R.S.M.
  10. 2/Lieut.Gillman.

"SECRET."   Copy No....1....

" 2ND BATTALION THE ROYAL MUNSTER FUSILIERS."
" OPERATION ORDER. No. 10 "

Reference Map Sheet 62c. N.E. 1/20,000.

1. The Battalion will relieve the 2nd Battn Roy Dublin Fusiliers, in the Line on the 10th instant.

2. The Battalion will march to the line in the following order :-
C, A, B, D, and Hd.Quarters.
Starting Point :- E.18.d.3.0.
ROUTE :- By Track to F.15.a.8.5.
Times :- C.Coy.at 5.p.m.   A.Coy.at 5.20.p.m.   B.Coy.at 5.40.p.m.
D.Coy.at 6.p.m.   Hd.Qr.Coy.at 6.20.p.m.
Dress :- Battle Order. Packs will be carried instead of Haversacks.
Movement will be by platoons at 500 yards interval.

3. 1.Guide per Coy will meet Battalion in road by Support Battn Hd.Qrs. F.15.a.8.5.
Platoon Guides will be at F.10.c.3.7., near Battn Hd.Quarters.

4. A.Coy 2nd R.M.Fus.will relieve C.Coy 2nd R.D.Fus.at GRAFTON POST.
C.Coy   "   "   A.Coy   "   at HEYTHORPE POST.
B.Coy   "   "   B.Coy   "   at MULE TRENCH POST
D.Coy   "   "   D.Coy   "   at(SAND BAG ALLEY, YAK
                                                                  (and ZEBRA POSTS.

5. Advance parties under 2nd Lieut.D.Welch, consisting of 2.N.C.Os.per Coy, 1.Cook per Coy, Nos.1.of Lewis Guns, Observers, and Signallers and 5. Stretcher Bearers will proceed to the line at 1.45.p.m.in the above order. No Group will consist of more than 4 men and there will be an interval of 25 yards between groups.

6. Blankets and Officers Kits will be stacked at the place where Rations are delivered by 10.30.a.m.
Haversacks, properly labelled, will be stacked by Coys at the same time and place.
Coys will collect their Caps and put them into Sand Bags properly labelled.
Lewis Gun Limbers will be loaded at the same place at 11.a.m.
Dixies and Trench Kits and Stores will be loaded at 3.p.m.

7. Patrol Orders will be issued separately.

8. Advance parties from the 10th Battn R.D.Fus will arrive forenoon to take over present Billets.
Billets will be handed over in a Clean and Sanitary state.
Certificates signed by the incoming Unit will be rendered to the Adjut.
Lieut.H.Darling will hand over all Stores,etc,to the 10th Battn R.D.F.

9. List of Trench Stores taken over to reach Battn Hd.Quarters by 8.a.m. 11th instant.

10. Completion of relief will be notified to battalion Hd.Quarters as heretofore.

11. ACKNOWLEDGE.

xxxxxxxxxxxxxxxxxxxxxxxxxxxxxxxxxxxxxxxxxxxxxxxxxxx xxxxx xxxxxxxxxxxxxx
Issued at _____ p.m.9.2.18.
                                                                                            Captain.

                Adjutant, 2nd Battalion The Royal Munster Fusiliers.

Copies to :-
No.1. War Diary.
   2. Office.
   3. A.Coy.
   4. B.Coy
   5. C.Coy
   6. D.Coy.
   7. Transport Officer.
   8. Qr.Master.
   9. R.S.M.
 10. Intelligence Officer.

SECRET.   Copy No. 1

2nd. Battn. The Royal Munster Fusiliers.
OPERATION ORDERS NO. 12.

Reference Map, LEMPIRE 1/10000.

1. The 2nd. Battn. The Roy. Munster Fus. will relieve 2nd. Battn. The Roy. Dublin Fus. in the line on the night 22/23rd. Feby.

2. "D" Coy. 2.R.M.F. will relieve "A" Coy. 2.R.D.F. in MULE TRENCH and COPSE.
   Coy. Hdqrs. at F.8.d.5.9.
   "B" Coy. 2.R.M.F. will relieve "C" Coy. 2.R.D.F. in OCKENDEN and RELIEF COPSE. Coy. Hdqrs. at F.2.b.3.8.
   "C" Coy. 2.R.M.F. will relieve "D" Coy. 2.R.D.F. in NORTH RESERVE.
   Coy. Hdqrs. at F.2.c.2.7.
   "A" Coy. 2.R.M.F. will relieve "B" Coy. 2.R/D.F. in TETARD WOOD.
   Coy. Hdqrs. at F.2.a.8.9.
   Starting Point; Present Coy. Hdqrs.
   Time.   6. p.m.

3. 4. guides per Coy. for "A" and "C" Coys. will be at Battn. Hdqrs. 2.R/D.F. at 5.45.p.m.
   4. guides per Coy. for "D" and "B" Coys. will be at MALASSISE FARM at 5.45.p.m.

   ~~A limber will be at "D" Coys. Hdqrs. at 4.15. p.m. for Lewis Guns and trench kits. These will be delivered at F.3.b.2.3.~~

4. An Officers' Patrol will be sent forward by "D" and "B" Coys. at 5.30.pm to cover the relief, and patrol region about W X.28.c.2.4. and X.27.d.0.5. These patrols will report to O.C. "A" and "C" Coys. 2.R.D.F. before going out. They will return at 10.p.m.

5. Advance parties of 1.Officer and 1.N.C.O. per Coy. the Regtl. Sergt. Maj. Observers, and Nos. 1. of Lewis Guns, will proceed to the line at 2.30.pm

6. Trench Stores, Defence Schemes, Work in hand and contemplated, will be taken over.

7. Blankets and officers' kits will be stacked at nearest point on main road to Coy. Hdqrs. at 4.30.p.m. A guard will be left by each Coy.

8. A limber will be at "D" Coys' Hdqrs. at 6:15.p.m. for Lewis Guns and trench kits. These will be delivered at F.3.b.2.3.

9. Billets will be handed over in a clean and sanitary condition, to advance parties of 2.R.D.F. and receipts obtained.

10. Relief of 2.R.D.F. will be notified by code word as formerly.

11. ACKNOWLEDGE.

Issued at 10 a.m.   Captain,
22nd; February 1918.   Adjutant, 2nd. Battn. The Royal Munster Fusiliers.

Copy No. 1. War Diary.
   "   " 2. Office.
   "   " 3. "A" Coy.
   "   " 4. "B" Coy.
   "   " 5. "C" Coy.
   "   " 6. "D" Coy.
   "   " 7? Quartermaster.
   "   " 8. Transport Officer.
   "   " 9. 2nd. Battn. Roy. Dub. Fus. (for information)
   "   " 10. 48th. Bde. (for information)

SECRET.   Copy No. 1.

2nd. Battn. The Royal Munster Fusiliers.

OPERATION ORDER NO. 11

Reference Map Sheet 62.C. N.E. 1/20000

1. The 2nd.Battn.The Royal Munster Fus.will be relieved in the line by the 1st.Battn.Royal Dublin Fus.on the night 18th/19th.Feby.

2. "A"Coy.2?R.M.F.will be relieved by "W"Coy.1st.R.D.F.in GRAFTON POST.
   "C"Coy.   "   "   "   "   "X"Coy.   "   "   in HEYTHROP POST.
   "B"Coy.   "   "   "   "   "Y"Coy.   "   "   in MULE TRENCH.
   "D"Coy.   "   "   "   "   "Z"Coy.   "   "   in SAND BAG ALLEY
                                                                 YAK and ZEBRA
                                                                 POSTS.

3. Guides (3.per Coy.)will be at Battn.Headqrs.at 5.45.p.m.

4. Advance parties from 1st.Roy.Dub.Fus.will arrive at 2.p.m.

5. All Trench Stores, Defence Schemes; work in hand and contemplated, will be handed over and receipts obtained. Aeroplane photographs will be retained. Trenches will be handed over in a clean and sanitary condition, and certificates obtained.

6. All Petrol Tins, Camp Kettles; and Trench Stores, brought in to the line will be sent out of the line at 3.p.m. and stacked by Coys.at the end of ST.PATRICK'S AVENUE.
   Battn.Headqrs.and Coys.will leave a guard in charge of Coy.Stores and Petrol Tins.

7. On relief Coys.will march to Support billets as follows:-
   "A"and "C"Coys.in cutting F.2.c.3.3.to F.2.c.1.8.Headqrs.of both Coys. in cutting. COPSE
   "D"Coy. MAY and ENFER WOOD Headqrs.at F.15.a.8.3.
   "B"Coy. MALASSISE FARM.
   Battn.Headqrs.at LEMPIRE F.15.a.90.35.

8. Coys.will send advance parties at 1.p.m. of 1.Officer and 3.N.C.O.s per Coy.to take over their billets,and Stores.They will thoroughly reconnoitre the new positions and will arrange to meet their Coys. and guide them to their billets.

9. Transport arrangements will be ;-
   Lewis Gun limbers at Battn.Dump F.10.a.5.3.at 6.15.p.m.
   Transport for Coy.Stores,Mess and Maltese Cart,at the end of ST.PATRICK'S AVENUE and Battn.Headqrs.at 6.p.m.

10. Completion of relief in the line will be notified by code wire as heretofore.
    Coys.will wire the same words to notify arrival in Support billets.

11. A C K N O W L E D G E .

Issued at 6.15 p.m.   Captain
                              Adjutant
17th.February.1918.   Comdg.2nd.Battn.The Royal Munster Fusiliers.

Copy No. 1?War Diary.
  "   " 2.Office.
  "   "3."A"Coy.
  "   "4."B"Coy.
  "   "5."C"Coy.
  "   "6."D"Coy.
  "   "7 Quartermaster.
  "   "8 Transport Officer.

48th Brigade.

16th Division.

Diary 1st to 20th March 1918 missing.

2nd BATTALION

THE ROYAL MUNSTER FUSILIERS

MARCH 1918

Appendices attached:-

Report from captured officer of the regiment

2nd Battn. The Roy. Munster Fusiliers 48
76

War Diary   MARCH, 1918

Thursday. 21st. At last the long expected enemy
offensive commenced.
The battalion was occupying
a series of positions between
EPÉHY and MALASSISE FARM.
The main position, called the
RIDGE RESERVE NORTH
running from MALASSISE
FARM on the right, to TETARD
WOOD on the left, was manned
by a portion "C" Coy., a portion
of "B" Coy. and all "D" Coy.
Two Strong Points in ROOM
TRENCH (otherwise evacuated)
about 200× in advance of RIDGE
RESERVE NORTH being manned
by one platoon of "C" Coy and
one platoon of "B" Coy.
The railway cutting EAST of
EPÉHY was manned by the
remainder of "B" Coy, Battn.
Headqrs. & one platoon of "C" Coy.
"A" Coy. were in reserve at the
cross roads S.W. of MALASSISE
FARM.

The officers of the battalion at this date were

Lieut-Col. H.R.H. IRELAND D.M.C.
　　　　3rd LEINSTER REGT. Cmdg.
Maj. M.M. HARTIGAN, D.S.O.
　　　　(GENERAL LIST)　　2nd i/c
Capt. F.S. WALDEGRAVE.　Adjutant
Lieut. W.W. MACKEOWN.　Asst. Adjt.
2 Lieut. H.H. STRACHAN　Sig. Officer
Lieut. McCARTNEY.　Liaison Officer
　　　127th Bde. R.F.A.
Lieut. J.B. STEWART.　　M.O.
　　　R.A.M.C.

"A" Coy
　Lieut. P.L. CAHILL.
2 Lieut. J.N. McINNES
　"　　P.M.J.A. ARDAGH

"B" Coy
　Capt. C.W. CHANDLER M.C.
2 Lieut. H.J. McELNEA
　"　　D.J. MEHEGAN
　"　　P.J. DENAHY

"C" Coy
　Lieut. H.G. WHELAN. M.C.
2 Lieut. M. TREACEY
　"　　J. DOORLEY
　"　　J.P. NASH.
Capt. D.R. HALL. (due to proceed on
　　　　　　　course of instruction

"D" Coy.
Lieut. W. S. KIDD
2/Lieut. P. A. MEYNAUD (K.O. MALTA. REGT)
2/Lieut L. A. CARTER

At Transport Lines.
Capt. B. H. PURDON.
Lieut. C. E. A. O'CALLAGHAN
2/Lieut T. ROCHE.   Transport Offr.

On courses of instruction
Capt. G. S. D. LANKTREE
2/Lieut J. W. GILLMAN
  "   H. G. COSGROVE
  "   W. O. VARIAN
  "   M. CLAIR

On leave to U.K.
Capt. P. W. NEWENHAM
2/Lieut J. P. O'CONNOR
  "   J. T. SHEFFIELD
  "   C. J. BERGIN
  "   J. P. MAY
  "   M. NUNAN
Rev. J. FLINN. C.F. Chaplain

× The enemy opened his bombardment at 4.30 a.m. with gas shells on the batteries and ordinary heavy shells on the trenches. The bombardment lasted for six hours, and a heavy white fog hung over our positions. Having rolled back the 66th Division "on our right, he outflanked the right battalion of our Brigade, who were obliged to fall back - leaving our right flank exposed, and he was able to attack MALASSISE FARM from the right rear, it falling into his hands before the garrison had a chance of putting up a serious fight. It was now about 11. am, and the fog had cleared somewhat. The Commanding officer having gone forward personally, to see how matters stood, was wounded and put out of action. Maj. M. M. HARTIGAN D.S.O. assumed command, and he moved Battn. Hdqrs. from the railway cutting near EPÉHY to a position 500x in the rear, and S.W. of EPÉHY.

The enemy having gained possession of RIDGE RESERVE NORTH, at the MALASSISE FARM end, he attacked down the trench with trench mortars, but it was not until 5. pm. that he succeeded in clearing the remnant of the garrison out of RIDGE RESERVE NORTH -

these joined up with the 8th LEICESTER RGT (21st Division) on our left.

Enemy infantry had by now advanced beyond LEMPIRE and were attacking along the LEMPIRE – EPÉHY road. They attacked Battn. Hdqrs. at 6 pm. and we were forced to move out, after a short sharp fight, in which Maj. HARTIGAN became "Missing". Battn. Hdqrs. moved to Bde Hdqrs in the Quarry. N. of ST. EMELIE. Meantime Capt. C.W. CHANDLER M.C. together with Lieut W.W. MacKEOWN, 2/Lt P.M.T.R. ARDAGH, and about 50 other ranks, held on to the railway cutting S.E. of EPÉHY. This party was pounded on the left by trench mortars, and a platoon of "C" Coy. on the left front cutting suffered severely, 2/Lt M. TREGEY being killed. The enemy now began to close in on the remnants of the battalion in the cutting, from the LEMPIRE – EPÉHY road, & taking advantage of the darkness the garrison withdrew by sections to EPÉHY and these joined up with the 8th LEICESTER REGT. at various strong points

Friday 22nd.

About 2 a.m. an order came through for all IRISH troops to withdraw to TINCOURT, which they reached in isolated parties during the day. The battalion was reduced from a trench strength of 629 other ranks to 290, and the following casualties occurred to officers on 21st inst.

Killed.
    Lieut. P. L. CAHILL
    " P. A. M. EYNAUD
    2/Lieut. M. TREACEY

Wounded (Hospital)
    Lt-Col. A. R. H. IRELAND. M.C.
    Capt. & Adjt. F. S. WALDEGRAVE

Wounded & Missing
    2/Lt. A. J. McELNEA.

Missing
    Maj. H. M. HARTIGAN. D.S.O
    Lieut. W. S. KIDD
    " H. G. WHELAN. M.C.
    2/Lieut. J. N. McINNES.
    " D. J. MEHEGAN
    " L. A. CARTER
    " P. J. DENAHY.

2/Lt. T. DOORLEY, with a few of his men, got back from their "Strong Point", accompanied by 2/Lt. J.F. NASH of this battn. who was attached to 48th T.M.B. This officer had lost his gun and team, in the attack. He remained with battn. Capt. B.H. PURDON + Lieut C.E.B. O'CALLAGHAN came up from Transport Lines. Capt. PURDON assuming command of the battn.

Saturday 23rd inst

During night 22/23rd battn took up a position at TINCOURT, behind the wood (Ref sheet 62.c. 17 b. and 18. a (approx)). The 11th HANTS. were on our right touching TINCOURT, and 2nd Roy. DUBLIN FUS. and 1st Roy. DUBLIN FUS. were on our immediate left, - the 47th BDE were on the left of our (48th BDE and the HQ 48th BDE, were in position 500 x EAST of our position
      With Capt D.P. HALL commanding "A" Coy. Lieut W.W. MacKEOWN "B" Coy, 2/Lt. P.M.J.A. ARDAGH "C" Coy, and

Lieut. C.E.A. O'CALLAGHAN "D" Coy, the battn. under orders withdrew to at 5.30 am, in the direction of DOINGT, in artillery formation. Here we took up a defensive position in an old trench running from DOINGT NORTH EAST, lying about J.30. The 1st & 2nd Roy. Dub. Fus., who occupied the high ground in front of us, withdrew through us, in face of advancing enemy about 2.30 p.m. The Bdes. on our right & left withdrew also, but the battn. held on for almost an hour, when the enemy in large numbers pressed very close. "A", "C", & "D" Coys withdrew towards FLAMICOURT, "B" Coy covering withdrawal.

The battn. passed through FLAMICOURT about 4.p.m. into PERONNE. Leaving PERONNE to take up a reserve position in H.36. central, it crossed the river SOMME as the Engineers were blowing up the last bridges.

Sunday 24th inst. At 2. am the battn was ordered to withdraw to CAPPY which was reached about 5.am here the men were billetted - the village was deserted. Major. H.B. TONSON-RYE (1st Roy. Munster Fus) joined the battn. and assumed command - from the staff of 34th Division.
Battn was reorganised - one company being formed with Capt C.W. CHANDLER. MC in command - four platoons were made.
Lieut W.W. McKEOWN appointed Acting/Adjt vice Capt + Adjt F.S. WALDEGRAVE (Hos/wounded)
At. 5.40 pm we left CAPPY + took up an Outpost position between R.3.c. and R.4. central (Ref. sheet 62.D), the 1st and 2nd Roy. Dub. Fus were on our right, and the 119th Bde on our left. It was reported that the enemy were advancing from the SOUTH and EAST, and the Bde was to guard the bridg

head at HALTE near FROISSY PILIER. No attack developed that night nor during the forenoon of 25th & the battn had ample time to search the district for derelict rations, which were found in plenty — we were at this time out of touch with our transport.

At 3.45 pm we returned to CAPPY, & took up positions on the CANAL LOCK & River Bridge N.E. of the village.

No enemy appeared.

Tuesday 26th.

On night 25th/26th orders received to blow up lock and bridges. This was done 6 am 26th. We withdrew from CAPPY at 10 am. "C" Coy under Capt D.P. Hall bringing up rear. Proceeded to "Point 81" WEST of CHUIGNOLLES & took up position from R.q.6.0.2. to R.q.6.0.0. Two Coys in Railway Cutting S.E. of this line. The 1st R.D.F. were in Support & enemy were engaged &

checked till 7 pm, when owing to heavy shell fire, & the retirement of our flanks, we withdrew to a line of trenches running NORTH & SOUTH in square R.6.7 where we remained till next day.
2.R.Dub.Fus on our right, 40th Bde on our left

Wednesday 21st.

Enemy made several attempts to push forward strong parties on our front, but was repulsed. In one of these bursts he succeeded in forcing the battn on our immediate left to evacuate their position, and began establishing himself there, but a small party of ours, gallantly and ably led by Lieut. CEA. O CALLAGHAN & RSM J. RING M.C. very soon drove the enemy out. In the afternoon Maj WHEELER (Cmdg 2. R.D.F) reported that he was out of with 47th Bde on his right. A rumour, after was despatched to locate 40th Bde HQ (two had been sent previously, but failed to return) He reported Bde had left.

A consultation was held by Comdg. Offrs. of units present viz 2nd. Roy Dub. Fus, South Irish Horse, & 2 Roy. Munster Fus.

The situation was held to be critical & it was decided to fall back. A further attempt was made to get into touch with Bde on our right but was unsuccessful.

2 R.D. ub. Fus. withdrew at 8. Km. followed by 2 R. Muns Fus. South Irish Horse were last to withdraw, covering withdrawal.

It was decided to withdraw via ECLUSIER BRIDGE, but as this was occupied by the enemy, the Column turned about, & marched down the towing path of the canal to CERISY. It was here found that the bridge was held by a

, German guard. These were shot, + the 3 battns doubled over the bridge + proceeded towards SAILLY LAURETTE on NORTH bank of the canal.

It was intended to cross the river to the NORTH, but we were fired on, when the river bridges were approached, so we again turned South, in order to recross the canal + work Westward, on the South Bank. Before reaching the Canal Bridge an officers Patrol (eight strong) was encountered, + as they appeared determined it was thought expedient to put them out of harms way, which was done, by rifle + revolver fire – The canal bridge was then crossed.

Thursday 28th

At about 1 am, the column was led westwards + eventually got into billets at HAMEL at 4 a.m. where Brig. Gen. RAMSEY visited us, and explained the situation. At 5am we "stood to" + at 10.am took up positions as Close Support in two sunken roads running EAST from HAMEL

Friday 29th.
The men made shelters, cleaned themselves, and rested

Saturday 30th.
2 Lieuts W.O. VARIAN, T.W. GILLMAN, and 2 other ranks joined us from transport lines. "Stood to" at 5am. Enemy put down a heavy bombardment lasting about one hour; + attacked at 10.am, when the batn advanced into the front line to assist CAREY'S FORCE in defending trenches. The attack was beaten off + the batn withdrew to its original position after dark

Casualties
 Capt. C.W. CHANDLER. MC Killed
 2 Lieut W.O. VARIAN Killed
 " J.W. GILLMAN Wounded

3. other ranks   killed.
15   "   "   wounded.
28   "   "   Missing.
Strength 3 offrs   90. other ranks

Sunday 31st. Quiet day - remained in
Support. Orders received to
take over Sector from CERISY
ROAD to CANAL. Capt
PURDON reconnoitred
the position

                    [signature]
                    - Major.

            Cmdg 2 Bn The Roy. Munster Fus

CONFIDENTIAL.   Ia/49833.C.

              COPY.   (40963)
                                          HOLZMINDEN,
                                          13th April, 1918.

I hope this will reach you: It has to follow an unusual route. I want you to communicate its contents to the Brigadier, who I sincerely hope is safe. If he has unfortunately been captured you had better send it to Col. WEBB at Division, as someone who cares must know how the 2nd Munsters ceased to exist. We appeared in no British communique but this is a quotation from the German one of 23.3.18:- "Heights of EPEHY captured after hard struggle in which the British were surrounded." Col. IRELAND was hit about 10.30 a.m.and I fear fatally. MALASSISE Farm was outflanked thro' old Copse and fell early but not without a most gallant resistance by its garrison. After my capture I was taken there and some German Staff Officers were most complimentary about Lieut. KIDD'S fine defence and regretted that he was severely wounded.

A Company had been ordered to counter-attack at MALASSISE Farm but Lieut. CAHILL was killed and I never succeeded in getting communication with the Company as it must have been cut off very early. With two companies wiped out, and realization of the weight of the enemy's attack I decided that the most effective fight I could put up would be to keep a wedge thrust forward into the enemy's advance while exposing to his attack as narrow a front as possible, and our battle formation which our brigade had directed us to take up in good time, two days before, made this feasible. By this time with the assistance of the fog, the enemy had broken into ROOM TRENCH and M post had fallen, but U post under Lieut. DOOLEY was doing great execution. I ordered Capt. CHANDLER with two platoons of B Company to make a strong point on the EPEHY side of the railway cutting close to the battalion aid post. When U post was taken about noon, Lieut. DOOLEY and a few survivors fell back on RIDGE RESERVE but what became of them eventually I don't know. The outstanding feature of our defence was the magnificent fight maintained throughout the day in RIDGE RESERVE and TETARD Wood by C Company and a few of B. The soul of this defence was Lieut. WHELAN M.G., who contested every bay in his trench and continued to rally and lead any men he could get hold of until noon on the following day. Lieut. Mc.E..RA? though suffering from a painful wound continued to fight until ordered back late in the day (21st). When the mist rose the enemy were discovered in mass in CATELET Valley and suffered severely at our hands. Rifle and M.G. fire from RIDGE RESERVE prevented the enemy from moving artillery up the MALASSISE road and every attempt up to 4 p.m. resulted in the horses and drivers being shot down and this effective fire was maintained in spite of the fact that in addition to repeated attacks on our right flank the enemy were engaging RIDGE RESERVE in reverse from MALASSISE Farm. By 4.30 p.m. the enemy assault troops had pressed Lieut. WHELAN back into the last two or three bays in TETARD Wood from where he side-stepped into the trench at the head of CATELET Valley.

The enemy were then closely investing the strong point in the railway cutting where Bn. H.Q. were when the battle commenced and as the capture of Lieut. WHELAN and his party appeared imminent I ordered him to fall back fighting on the ruins of EPEHY and with the survivors of B Company continued to dispute possession of the village with the enemy. B. Company under Capt.

                                                          /CHANDLER

CHANDLER in the point had done fine execution the day than anything else prevented the advance from MALASSISE Farm. The unit sent up to our support on that flank was tied down by the enemy's fire to the railway line and did not deploy sufficiently to the left to get touch with us though this unit doubtless found a few stragglers of D. or A. companies lining the embankment. Through the gap thus left the enemy eventually forced his way drove back the unit referred to and practically surrounded our position. So much I expected sooner or later but hoped that it would not occur before nightfall. In any case we could fight on while our ammunition lasted but we had used an enormous quantity. In falling back on EPEHY my intention was to reinforce the unit in that position and if eventually driven out to make our last stand in the YELLOW LINE and the village. From there I had been able to keep up communication throughout the day with B. and C. companies and with Brigade by runner. About 6 p.m. while giving the adjutant some instructions a man on look-out duty reported that the Germans were just outside the dug-out. I ordered everyone to get into the trench (YELLOW LINE) where I expected to find the troops who had been garrisoning it throughout the day under comparatively easy conditions. I led the way out of the dug-out and on reaching the duck-board I at once saw a group of the enemy standing on top of the dug-out. A German officer covered me with his revolver but I dodged and shouting "come on" ran for the trench. On reaching it I turned to the left and to my surprise found the enemy in the next bay. The garrison had left the trench without even warning me though I had been in touch with the platoon commander all day and had lent him a Lewis gun. I doubled back and seeing no sign of any of my own people concluded that on the taking of the trench they had gone to the right which would be the safer direction. It was getting dark and a party of troops I took to be ours turned out to be enemy. I was captured. Lieut. WHELAN and 2nd Lieut. DENNEHY? held out in EPEHY until noon next day when they joined me as prisoners having fired their last round and thrown the last bomb before surrendering. I wish I knew what happened to Capt. WALDEGRAVE, Lieut. STRACHAN and R.S.M. KING. The first-named rendered splendid service but I suppose if he was captured instead of killed nothing can be done for him. Same with WHELAN. I know that CHANDLER and CAHILL were killed. KIDD severely wounded and prisoner. WHELAN and DENNEHY prisoners. Enemy aircraft gave us a bad time. C. Company brought one down in a trench with Lewis gun fire. One of the men brought another down with a single shot with his rifle; killed the pilot. The battalion runners did splendidly. See the people at home do what they can for our men who are prisoners. The officers will be alright. Hope you got our kits away. If you did try and hurry them home to COX so that our people can get at them. Take a copy of this please and keep it for me. Write me all the news you can. You will probably have heard of some of the fellows I can't account for.

M.M.H.

2nd R Munster Fus

April 1918

16/28

Vol 37

War Diary
of
2nd R. Munster Fus
for
Month of April 1918

Army Form C. 2118.

WAR DIARY
or
INTELLIGENCE SUMMARY.

(Erase heading not required.)

2/R.M.F

Instructions regarding War Diaries and Intelligence Summaries are contained in F. S. Regs., Part II. and the Staff Manual respectively. Title pages will be prepared in manuscript.

Place	Date	Hour	Summary of Events and Information	Remarks and references to Appendices
AMIENS HAMEL	1-4-18		The Battalion remained in support to the 1st and 2nd R. DUBLIN FUSRS and to "CAREY'S FORCE". The day passed quietly.	
	2.4.18		At 10.30 p.m. the Baton. relieved "CAREY'S FORCE" in the front line N of CERISY ROAD - the 1st R DUBLIN FUS. being on our right and the 2nd R. DUBLIN FUS in our left. The 2nd R. IRISH REGT took over from us in the support line. A quiet day.	
	3.4.18		A very quiet day except for a little sniping on our side and some shelling from the Enemy. At 10.40 p.m. the Battalion was relieved by the 9th Rifle Brigade, and marched out of the trenches Westwards. On reaching AUBIGNY a halt was made for a hot meal. Eight Kilometres beyond AUBIGNY at a pond on the AMIENS Road the Battalion entrained for SALEUX which was reached at 6 a.m. 2 Lt THORNLEY rejoined	

Army Form C. 2118.

WAR DIARY
or
INTELLIGENCE SUMMARY.
(Erase heading not required.)

Place	Date	Hour	Summary of Events and Information	Remarks and references to Appendices
AMIENS MAP DIEPPE MAP	3/4/18		The Battalion today from leave in SALEUX until 4pm when it entrained for BLANGY which was reached at 11pm	
	4/4/18		The Battalion moved off at 1am for VILLEROY arriving at VILLEROY at 3.30 it was found that there was very poor accommodation in this village details of the 39th DIVISION occupied most of the streets it was subsequently discovered that the Battalion should have gone to RAMBURES and it was decided to move there next day	APPENDIX A 48 INF BDE Report on Operations from 21.3.18 to 4.4.18 inclosed

Army Form C. 2118.

WAR DIARY
or
INTELLIGENCE SUMMARY.
(Erase heading not required.)

Instructions regarding War Diaries and Intelligence Summaries are contained in F. S. Regs., Part II, and the Staff Manual respectively. Title pages will be prepared in manuscript.

Place	Date	Hour	Summary of Events and Information	Remarks and references to Appendices
RAMBURES	5/4/18		At 11am today the battalion left VILLEROY for RAMBURES to take up new billets. Plenty of accommodation was found in the village. The men occupied the remainder of the day in cleaning up & resting.	
"	6/4/18		Battalion Orders were issued today for the first time since the 9th Feby. There was a General inspection of Arms, equipment, clothing etc. with a view to making up all deficiencies. Coys were re-organised on the Platoon basis. Lieut Newton & 2 Lieuts J.P. May and C.T. Bergin rejoined the Battn from leave.	
"	7-4-18		Today (Sunday) the battalion handed fuel & length for the R.C. service at 10am. Baths & clean clothing were provided for the men & the Divisional Gas N.C.O. inspected all Box Respirators.	
"	8-4-18		The Battalion remained in billets. Under authority granted by His Majesty the King, Captain D.P. HALL 5th attd 2nd Royal Munster Fusiliers	

Army Form C. 2118.

WAR DIARY
or
INTELLIGENCE SUMMARY.
(Erase heading not required.)

Instructions regarding War Diaries and Intelligence Summaries are contained in F. S. Regs., Part II. and the Staff Manual respectively. Title pages will be prepared in manuscript.

Place	Date	Hour	Summary of Events and Information	Remarks and references to Appendices
RAMBURES	2-4-18		has been awarded the Military Cross for gallantry and devotion to duty in the field	a.a. 5th army
			Major H.B. TONSON-RYE resumed command of the Battalion vice Lieut Col	A/G/15/30/4/30
			H.R.H. IRELAND M.C. (Casualty in action) with effect from the 24th March 1918	
			Major H.B. TONSON-RYE is permitted to wear the badges of rank of Lieut.	
			Colonel whilst commanding the Battalion	
			Capt V.D. O'MALLEY M.C. Royal Irish Fusiliers attached for duty to the	
			Battalion took over the duties of Adjutant with effect from the 1st April 1918	
			Capt C.R. HEFFERNAN RAMC posted to the Battalion with effect from the	
			3rd April 1918 assumed today the duties of Bth. Medical Officer.	
			Lieut J. ROCHE assumed the duties of Bth. Transport Officer vice Lieut	
			M.J. RYAN M.C. (in hospital wounded)	
			The following Officers of the Royal Irish Fusiliers are posted to the Battalion	
			and reported for duty today:- 2/Lieut G. BARRY; 2/Lieut C.G. CRADDOCK	
			2/Lt. J.F. WILKES; 2/Lieut B.J. DAVIES; 2/Lieut M.R. FEEHAN.	
Ref. Map.	9-4-18		In accordance with Bth. OO No 21 the Battalion marched to EMBREVILLE	
DIEPPE			leaving RAMBURES at 9.30 a.m. and arriving in billets at EMBREVILLE at 2.30 p.m.	
ABBEVILLE				

WAR DIARY
or
INTELLIGENCE SUMMARY.
(Erase heading not required.)

Army Form C. 2118.

Instructions regarding War Diaries and Intelligence Summaries are contained in F.S. Regs., Part II. and the Staff Manual respectively. Title pages will be prepared in manuscript.

Place	Date	Hour	Summary of Events and Information	Remarks and references to Appendices
Ref Maps ABBEVILLE HAZEBROUCK 5m	10-4-18		In accordance with B.M. OO No 23 the Battalion marched to WOINCOURT leaving at 10am and arriving at the Railway Station at 11:15am. After dinner the Battalion entrained and proceeded to WIZERNES detraining there at 10 p.m. The Battalion then marched to WAVRANS arriving in billets there at 2.30 p.m. (11-4-18).	
	11-4-18		The Battalion left WAVRANS at 9.30 am and marched to HAPPE. Two companies were billeted at Le Val RESTANT. The following Officers of the 19th Entrenching Battalion joined the Battalion today :— CAPT. F.W. SYNNOTT, 2nd LIEUT. J. OWENS. CAPT. SYNNOTT took over command of "D" Coy. Companies were occupied during the day in re-organ- ising, inspection of kits and cleaning up. The Commanding Officer inspected the Battalion at 3 p.m.	
HAPPE	12-4-18		The G.O.C. 48th Infantry Brigade inspected the Battalion at 10 a.m. at CAMPAGNE LES BOULONNAIS. Major C.E. SMYTHE. joined the Battalion today. Captain C.J.D.	
"	13.4.18			

Army Form C. 2118.

WAR DIARY
or
INTELLIGENCE SUMMARY.
(Erase heading not required.)

Place	Date	Hour	Summary of Events and Information	Remarks and references to Appendices
Ref map HAZEBROUCK 5G	13-4-18		LANKTREE rejoined the Battalion for duty with Lewis Gun Batt. 2nd Lt. J.T. SHEFFIELD rejoined from leave. At 2 pm orders were received to move at once to new billets. The Battalion left HAPPE at 3 pm and marched to SENLECQUES arriving there 5.45 pm. Orders were received that the 1st Battalion R Munster Fusiliers and the 2nd Battalion R Munster Fusiliers were to form a Composite Battalion in the 16th Div Composite Inf. Brigade. The Battalion to be commanded by Lt Col H.B. Towson. R/F with the present HQrs of 2nd R.M.F.	
CALAIS 13	14-4-18		Orders were received at 7.45 am to march to INGHEM. During the march the Battalion was re-organised into 2 Companies, and 2 Companies were attached from the 1st Batt. R. Munster Fus. The Coys were called Nos 1, 2, 3, 4 Coys. The strength of the Composite Battalion was Officers — 28 — O.Rs. 896. The Battalion arrived at	

Army Form C. 2118.

WAR DIARY
or
INTELLIGENCE SUMMARY.
(Erase heading not required.)

Place	Date	Hour	Summary of Events and Information	Remarks and references to Appendices
HAZEBROUCK So. Map	14-4-18		INGHEM at 4.45 pm and billeted there for the night	
	15-4-18	6.30 pm	In accordance with Brigade Order 14.4.18 the Composite Battalion left INGHEM at 9am and marched to STEENBECQUE arriving there at 3.30 pm	
			Orders were received that the Brigade was to be employed on digging a new defensive line, that portion allotted to the Battalion reaching from I 16 Central to I 5 C 4.2	16th Div Comp INF.BRG.O.No2
			Ref. Sheet 36a 1/40.000	
STEENBECQUE	16-4-18		The Battalion commenced work on the new line at 1 pm today and continued until 7.15 pm two being taken on the ground. The task allotted for the day was a trench 5' x 3' and 75% of this took was completed. The organization and equipment of the Battalion was carried out at every available moment. A large quantity of clothing and articles of equipment were issued today, and Battle Stores were	

Army Form C. 2118.

WAR DIARY
or
INTELLIGENCE SUMMARY.
(Erase heading not required.)

Instructions regarding War Diaries and Intelligence Summaries are contained in F. S. Regs., Part II. and the Staff Manual respectively. Title pages will be prepared in manuscript.

Place	Date	Hour	Summary of Events and Information	Remarks and references to Appendices
HAZEBROUCK SOUMAR STEENBECQUE	16-4-18		Party made up.	
	17-4-18		The Battalion at full strength recommenced work on the new line at 9am and continued until 3pm with dinners on the ground. Conferences continued with equipping in the evening. Lieut T.P. Reynolds 1st Batt. R. Munster Fusiliers reported for duty with the Composite Battalion.	
	18-4-18		The Battalion was occupied today in continuing digging of the new line. Hours of work were from 9am to 3pm at the end of the days work the trench had been dug to a depth of 3' and a width of 6'; parapets and parados were constructed. Orders were received today for a fresh re-organisation of the Battalion, on the following lines. The Battalion HQrs. and transport of the 1st Battalion R. Munster Fus. and the personnel of the 1st and 2nd Batts R. Munster Fus. less a training	16th Div Comp INF Bde Adm. O. No 2

Army Form C. 2118.

WAR DIARY
or
INTELLIGENCE SUMMARY.
(Erase heading not required.)

Instructions regarding War Diaries and Intelligence Summaries are contained in F. S. Regs., Part II. and the Staff Manual respectively. Title pages will be prepared in manuscript.

Place	Date	Hour	Summary of Events and Information	Remarks and references to Appendices
HAZEBROUCK MAP STEENBECQUE	18.4.18		Staff consisting of 10 officers and 42 o.r. of the 2nd Batt R. Munster Fus. and the Transport of the 2nd Batt R. Muns-TER Fus, to form one Battalion.	
	19.4.18		Battalion H.Qrs and Transport of the 1st Batt R. Munster Fus. arrived at STEENBECQUE and the new organization was completed during the day. A Conference of Commanding Officer of the 16th DIVISIONAL COMPOSITE INF. BRIGADE was held at 10 a.m and met ag am at 3 p.m. The Conference was held for the purpose of discussing the formation of the Training Staff and Establishment of the Battalions intended for training purposes, The following is a roll of the Officers included in the Training Staff of the 2nd R Munster Fus:- Lt Col H B Towson-Rye Commanding Officer Major B H Purdon Captain V D O'Malley M.C. A/Adjutant	

WAR DIARY
INTELLIGENCE SUMMARY

Army Form C. 2118.

Place	Date	Hour	Summary of Events and Information	Remarks and references to Appendices
HAZEBROUCK MAP STEENBECQUE	19.4.18		CAPT. C.C. SMYTHE, CAPT. C.J.D. LANKTREE, LIEUT. W.W. MACKEOWN, 2nd LIEUT. J.T. SHEFFIELD, 2nd LIEUT. D.J. DAVIES, 2nd LIEUT. J. OWENS, 2nd LIEUT. G. BARRY. The 42 O.Rs. that formed the Training Establishment included the Regt. Sergt. Major, Regt. Q.M.S., 4 Coy Sergt. Majors and 4 Coy QMS. The Transport Consisted of Lieut. T. ROCHE Transport Officer and 42 O.Rs. In accordance with instructions the Baton	
	20.4.18		Transport moved back at 3pm to WAVRANS. The personnel of the Battalion, other than that forming the Training Establishment and the Transport left today with the 1st Batt R Munster Fus.	16th Div Comp. Inf Base Inst No 5
	21.4.18		Orders were received this morning to move back to WAVRANS. March was commenced at 3pm. Billets 10am and INGHEM was reached for the night. were obtained here for the night.	

Army Form C. 2118.

WAR DIARY
or
INTELLIGENCE SUMMARY.

(Erase heading not required.)

Instructions regarding War Diaries and Intelligence Summaries are contained in F. S. Regs., Part II. and the Staff Manual respectively. Title pages will be prepared in manuscript.

Place	Date	Hour	Summary of Events and Information	Remarks and references to Appendices
HAZEBROUCK on map	22.4.18		The march was resumed at 10 a.m. and the Battn arrived at WAVRANS at 12 noon. 2nd C BARRY attended a Lewis Gun demonstration at CAMIERS. The following Officers reported this evening to the 2nd Army Musketry School to attend a four days Course:- Major B.H. PURDON, CAPT. C.O. LANKTREE, Capt. C.C. SMYTHE, Lieut. W.W. MACKEOWN, 2nd Lt. J.T. SHEFFIELD, 2nd Lt. G. BARRY. The W.O. and N.C.O. instructional staff also attended this Course.	
WAVRANS	23.4.18		The Commanding Officer visited the 2nd Army Musketry School. The details remaining in billets were paraded under R.S.M.	
	24.4.18		With all Officers and the N.C.O. instructional staff at the 2nd Army Musketry School only a parade of all details in billets took place today.	
	25.4.18		The G.O.C. 48th Infantry Brigade inspected	

WAR DIARY
or
INTELLIGENCE SUMMARY.
(Erase heading not required.)

Army Form C. 2118.

Place	Date	Hour	Summary of Events and Information	Remarks and references to Appendices
HAZEBROUCK to WAVRANS	25.4.18		The Battalion transport today. Orders were received this morning to move to new area at 2 p.m. The lorries moved off at 2 p.m. and were allotted billets in VAUDRINGHEM which was reached at 4.30 p.m.	
	26.4.18		All Officers and N.C.O.'s at the 2nd Army Musketry School returned today. Orders were received for Commanding Officers to make a reconnaissance of the training area and submit a programme of work for the training staff for the week commencing 29th April.	
	27.4.18		Parade of all W.O.s, NCOs men at 10 a.m. under the R.S.M. Company Commanders were engaged in drawing up a tactical scheme for submission to Brigade.	
	28.4.18		Church Parades were held today. R.C. parade at 10.30 am C.of E. parade at 12 noon. There were no other parades during the day.	
	29.4.18		The training of the Instructional Staff Commenced	

Army Form C. 2118.

WAR DIARY
or
INTELLIGENCE SUMMARY.
(Erase heading not required.)

Place	Date	Hour	Summary of Events and Information	Remarks and references to Appendices
HAZEBROUCK Sur MER VAUDRINGHEM	29.4.18		Today a tactical scheme was carried out on ground near FLOYECQUES.	
	30.4.18		Training in accordance with programme was continued today.	

2-5-18.

Honor/p Lieut Colonel
Cmdg 2nd R. Munster Fus.

Diary of 2nd Munsters - April 1918.

APPENDIX A

48th INFANTRY BRIGADE.   G.53/1.
2nd Bn Royal Munster Fusiliers.

"REPORT ON OPERATIONS FROM 21.3.1918 to 4.4.1918 inclusive;"

Reference Sheets 62.C.and 62.D. 1/40,000.

1918.
21st March.

At 4.30.a.m.the Enemy opened a Bombardment with Gas Shells and 5.9s'on the Battle Zone, and as farr back as Brigade Hd Qrs.

At 6.30.a.m.the enemy increased the intensity of his bombardment with Guns of heavy calibre. About 6.a.m.as dawn broke a very heavy mist/hung over our positions, this together with the smoke and the bombardment made it impossible to see more than 5 yards in front of one.

At about 9.30.a.m.when the fog was beginningto lift slightly the bombardment slackened.

At 9.45.a.m.the enemy appeared on the LEMPIRE-CATELET road, a fight ensued between them and the remnents and the garrison of the trenches astride the road. The enemy at this point were held back until 12.30.p.m.; two Vickers Guns and several Lewis Guns remaining in action for that time.

About 10.a.m.a party of the enemy obtained a footing in our front line trench bout MAY COPSE. All counter attackes to dislodge them failed.

About 11.30.a.m.it appears that two platoons holding the front line astride the LEMPIRE-CATELET road were overwhelmed as none returned to the ridge, all garrisons of strong points would appear to have been overwhelmed as none returned.

At this time the enemy had penetrated to RONSSOY and established himself on the W.end of the village.

Troops of the Brigade on our Right were seen falling back through RONSSOY WOOD.

At about 12 noon the enemy put down a barrage along the valley between RIDGE SUPPORT and RONSSOY WOOD. The Brigade on our Right withdraw to the BROWN LINE and the enemy pursuing established themselves in a portion of the RAPERIE SWITCH.

At 12.15. p.m.the enemy established themselves on the LEMPIRE-EPHE Y road and with M.Gs' drove out Centre Battalion (1st R.Dub.Fus).back to the BROWN LINE. Our Right Battalion the 2nd R.Dub.Fus.having both flanks in the air was compelled to withdraw under very heavy M.G.fire into the BROWN LINE.

The enemy now attacked MALASSISE FARM from the Right Rear before the garrison had a chance to put up a serious fight.

The enemy now attacked down the trench with T.Ms! towards on our left Battalion. The troops holding these trenches held out until 6.p.m. The Right Flank being cut off, they were compelld to withdraw unto the Right Battalion of Brigade on Left (8th. Leicesters,21st Division). The C.O.and the 2nd in Command and all other Officers of the Battalion(2nd R.Munster Fusiliers) except 2/Lieuts' Dooley and Nash, had by this time become casualties.

At 3.p.m.the 48th Infantry Brigade less 2nd Royal Munster Fusiliers and the 49th Infantry Brigade were on the BROWN LINE.

All details,H.Q.Staff,and T.M.Battery were sent forward to reinforce the BROWN LINE and orders were issued to hold on to it at all costs.

About 3.p.m.6th Connaught Rangers of the 47th Infantry Bde with 2 Tanks passed through the BROWN LINE with the object of Counter attacking the BOES SWITCH. This attacked failed, the Tanks returned with the Connaught Rangers.

From 4.P.M.till dusk the enemy maintained avery heavy barrage on the BROWN LINE and area immediately in rear. At the same time the hostile Air-craft flew very low shooting at our men in the trenches.

About 6.p.m.the enemy had established his M.Gs! in forward position in front of the BROWN LINE, and the ground between the BROWN LINE and VILLERS FAUCON was swept by M.G.fire.

About 6. p.m.O.C. 47th Inf.Bde.assumed command of the BROWN LINE S.of the ROISEL-EPEHY Railway.

At midnight orders were received for all IRISH Trops to withdraw to TINCOURT.

BATTALION ORDERS.

BY

LIEUT-COL.H.B.TONSON-RYE.COMMANDING.2ND BATTALION THE ROYAL MUNSTER FUSILIERS

In the Field.　　　　　　　　M O N D A Y.　　　　　　　　22nd April,1918.

P A R T.1. No. 36.

Battalion Orders Part 1.were last issued on 12th April,1918.

1. **ROUTINE.**　　Reveille tomorrow will be at

22nd March.   Dispositions as per attached Map.

23rd March.   The Brigade remained in these positions until 5.30.a.m.23d inst, when orders were received to withdraw to a Defensive position E.of DOINGT. This withdrawl was carried out in perfect order in succession of Battalions. A very thick fog prevailed. The connection was kept up between Brigade H.Qrs. and Battalions by connecting files at 100 yards interval. On arriving at BUIRE the fog lifted and Battalions moved to positions allotted by map " " attached. Brigade was in position at 9.30.a.m.
    At about 10.30.a.m. enemy in skirmishing order were seen advancing towards our position. At 11.a.m. his Field Artilley opened on our lines. At 1.p.m. troops on our left were seen withdrawing, and a message was received from 49th Inf.Brigade asking us to cover their withdrawl through PERONNE. Shortly after this two Battalions of the Brigade on our left were seen withdrawing. The Officer Commanding the Support Battaln (2nd R.Dub.Fusiliers) immediately moved up his Battalion to occupy the trenches vacated by this Brigade. The Reserve Battalion (1st R.Dub.Fusiliers) was ordered to take up a position facing E. to protect our Right Flank, which was obscure, and to cover the withdrawl of the remainder of the Brigade. An order was then issued to withdraw by Battalions from the Left after covering the withdrawl of the 49th Inf. Brigade and to take up a position on the MAISONETTE RIDGE, vide Map " ".
    During the withdrawl, Lewis Guns were left in positions from which they could delay the enemys' advance. The Bridges were blown immediately our troops had crossed the river.
    At 10/30.p.m. the 39th Division having taken over the line held by our troops, orders were issued to withdraw to CAPPY.

24th March.   The morning was spent in reorganising Units. About 5.P.M orders were received to take up an outpost position facing S. to guard the Bridge Head at FROISSY. 49th Inf Brigade were on our Right, 39th Division on our Left.
    Dispositions as per attached Maps.

25th March.   About 1.p.m. orders were received that the 16th (IRISH) Division had been transferred from the VII. to the XIXth. Corps. The River SOMME being the dividing line between Corps. The Role of the Brigade was to guard the line of the SOMME RIVER and the CANAL on the Left Flank of the XIX. Corps, from a possible attack from the North. 39th Divn were on the Right and 49th Inf.Bde on the Left.
    Dispositions are shewn on attached Map " ". The Bde was in position by 5.p.m.

26th March.   Orders were received that if seriously pressed the XIX. Corps would withdraw fighting to the line (ROUVROY-PROYART)-FROISSY). Orders were issued for all crossings to be held by our troops so long as line held by 39th Division remained E.of them.
    Touch was maintained with the Left Battalion of the 39th Division which withdrew about 7.a.m., consequently the Battalions under my command withdrew in succession towards CHUIGNOLLES; where a position was taken up in accordance with orders received. Dispositions are shewn on attached Map" "
    The 47th Inf.Brigade on the Right Flank and the 49th on the Left Flank. The Brigade was in position about 12 noon.
    About 4.p.m. the enemy commenced to attack. Rifle and M.G.fire was opened on both sides. About 5.p.m. the enemy brought up Field Artillery and fired over direct sights at our positions.
    Later on 4.2s'and 5.9s' came into action.
    It was reported that the enemy were massing in CHUIGNOLL and the heavy and all available Artillery were asked to concentrate on that village. The fire was very effective and delayed the advance of the enemy.
    About 7.p.m. the troops on our Left withdrew, thus allowing the enemy to obtain a footing in the Railway from

Whence they enfiladed our troops occupying that position, causing them to retire to a positions as shewn on Map " ", in conjunction with 49th Inf.Brigade on our Left.

A Company of the 11th Hampshire Pioneers were then sent up to fill up the gap thus caused between the 47 Inf.Brigade and 48th Inf.Brigade.

Orders were issued to hold this position at all costs.

27th March.

At dawn the enemy made several attempts to push forward strong parties along our front;these were all repulsed.

He succeeded however in forcing the Battalion on our immediate Left(2nd Rl.Irish.Regt) to evacuate their position and began to establish himself. A Counter Attack led by Lieut. O'Callaghan and R.S.M. Ring,M.C.2nd Rl.Munster Fusiliers successfully drove the enemy out.

It now became evident that the main line of the Enemys' advance was along the main road and up the valley towards MORCOURT. Troops could be seen advancing and a Battery of Artillery came into action in R.15.a. About 3.p.m. 3 out of their 4 guns were forced to withdraw and considerable casualties were caused by our Rifle and M.G.fire.

About 2.p.m. a message was received from the 47th Inf.Bd. saying they were unable to hold on and were going to withdraw into MORCOURT.

Shortly after this a Company of the 11th Hampshire Pionee which had been sent to get touch with the 47th Inf.Brigade and some details of the 39th Division,being pressed by the Enemy began to withdraw. Theses were collected and sent back to hold a line about Q.18.central facing East. It was now evident that the enemy was advancing rapidly on MORCOURT along the MORCOURT-PROYART ROAD.

A Battalion of the 39th Division(13th Gloster Pioneers) who were withdrawing were ordered by me to hold their ground together with a Company of the 11th Hants to delay the enemy advance and cover the withdrawl of the 48th and 49th Inf.Brigades. A message was at once sent to G.O.C.49th Inf. Bde.informing him of the situation and as his only line of withdrawl was threatened it was suggested that he should commence withdrawing from his Left Flank under cover of my Brigade. I subsequently went over to see the G.O.C.49th Inf Brigade who informed me that he had ordered all troops to withdraw ing succession from the Left.

I sent up Runners to my Battalions with orders to withdraw and take up positions in Q.9.and Q.15.central after the Battalions of the 49th Inf.Brigade had withdrawn. Only one of these Runners succeeded in reaching one of the Battalion (1st Rl.Dublin Fusiliers).

About 3.15.p.m.it was reported to me that the 49th Inf. Brigade and 1st and 2nd R.D.Fus.had passed along the CANAL BANK to the North of MORCOURT. I then ordered my Briga Major to proceed after them and form them up on the position assigned to them. This Officer never returned to me and is still missing.

About 4.p.m.I took up my positions about Q.22.central. The troops of the 49th Division were then withdrawing through me. The enemy had now established himself with M.Gs.on the Southern Bank of the River about Q.14.and 20.central,driving our troops into the LA MOTTE-SANTERRE Road,where they were reorganised and took up a position W.of WARFUSSE-APANCOURT joining up with CAREY'S Details in the BOIS DE TAILLOUS. In the meanwhile the enemy had pressed into MORCOURT entirely cutting off the remnants of the 2nd Rl.Dublin Fus.,2nd Rl. Munster Fusiliers.and S.I.H.(48th Inf.Bde),in all about 200 men.

These troops held their positions until dark when a reconnaissance of the river was made by Capt.STITT,2nd Rl. Dub.Fusiliers.,and all Bridges were found to be occupied by the enemy. It was then decided to rush the German Guard holding the Bridge Head at CERISY. The counter sign having been learnt the party marched through in fours on to the Bridge which had only been partially destroyed.

The guard was overwhelmed and killed and the party proceeded along North Bank to SAILLY-LAURETT where hostile guards were again encountered. These were dealt with in a similar manner and the party reached HAMEL where it joined up with the remainder of the Brigade.

28th March. The Brigade was ordered to take up a position in Support to CAREY'S Force E. of HAMEL. 49th Inf. Brigade were on Right Flank, 11th Hants on Left Flank, vide Map " ".

29th March. The troops remained in the same position. The enemy opened a heavy bombardment about 4.30.p.m., but no attack was seen to develope. A party of details 500 strong under Major. Heffernan M.C., came under my command, and took up a position in Reserve in BOIS-de-VAIRE.14.d.

30th March. At 11.30.a.m. the enemy opened a very heavy bombardment along the whole line, and at 12 noon the barrage lifted unto a position in rear about the line of our Supports. At the same time he launched his attack.

The Support Battalions in accordance with orders moved forward clear of the barrage to a position in immediate support. About 12.20.p.m. troops were seen coming away from the FRONT LINE where the enemy had succeeded in penetrating. All Support Battalions counter-attacked and re-occupied the Front Line.

Elements of the enemy remained in Shell-holes close to the front line and in isolated trench immediately in front until about 1.15. p.m. when he was finally driven off. Troops remained in their position until dark, when the Front Line was re-organised and a number of the Supports withdrawn to their original position.

31st March. Orders were received to take over from the Cavalry from P.10.central to the River SOMME, vide Map " ".
The Details under Major.H.Heffernan were ordered to rejoin their Units.

1st April. No change.

2nd April. Orders were received for CAREY'S Force to be withdrawn, and the Front was held with three Battalions of the 48th Inf. Brigade. in line, with three Battalions of the 49th Inf.Bde. in Support.

3rd April. On the Night of 3rd/4th April, the 16th Division was relieved by the 14th Division.

4th April. In conclusion I wish to place in record my appreciation of the magnificent spirit and fighting qualities shown by all during the period covered by this report.

The very heavy casualties inflicted on the enemy in the Battle Zone on the 21-3-1918, and the strenght of the Units coming out of action on that day (total in the Brigade :- 16.Officers and 600 other ranks) will suffice to show the severity of the fighting.

The withdrawl on the subsequent days could not have been carried out in a more orderly and soldierly like manner, and reflects the greatest credit on all ranks.

On no occasion did the Brigade withdrew from its position until its flanks had been turned and its line of retreat threatened.

The courage and determination displayed by all ranks in the successful repulse of the enemy's attack East of HAMEL, 30-3-18, after continuous fighting for 9 days and immediately following a period of 46 days continuously in the trenches, would maintain the highest traditions of the IRISH race and the fighting qualities of the IRISH Soldier.

Casualties from 21.3.18. to 4.4.18. were :—

	OFFICERS.	O.RANKS.
1st Rl. Dublin Fusiliers	38.	731.
2nd Rl. Dublin Fusiliers	45.	827.
2nd Royal Munster Fusiliers	36.	796.

Strength of Units on coming out of action on 4.4.1918:—

	OFFICERS.	O.RANKS.
1st Rl. Dublin Fusiliers	7.	217.
2nd Rl. Dublin Fusiliers	5.	204.
2nd Royal Munster Fusiliers	3.	142.

8th April, 1918.   (Sgd). F. RAMSAY. BRIG-GENERAL.
Commanding 48th Infantry Brigade.

2nd
R. Munster Fus
May 1918

WAR DIARY
INTELLIGENCE SUMMARY.
(Erase heading not required.)

Army Form C. 2118.

2 R Munster 2nd B/34

Place	Date	Hour	Summary of Events and Information	Remarks and references to Appendices
Rd Mm HAZEBROUCK 5" VAUDRINGHEM	1918 May 1		Training was carried out in accordance with attached programme	App. I
			2/Lieut. T. J. SHEFFIELD proceeded on a course of Instruction at 1st Army Scouting Observation and Sniping School	
"	2		Training was carried out in accordance with attached programme	
			2/Lieut. C. BARRY proceeded on a Lewis Gun course at 1st Army School of Instruction	
"	3		Training was carried out in accordance with attached programme	
			The XIX" Corps Commander has awarded the following decorations for acts of Gallantry in the Field :-	
			No 10543 C.S.M. J. STRONNER Bar to Military Medal.	
			" 5734 Sgt. H. TRACEY Military Medal.	
			" 8242 L/Cpl J. GALLAGHER Military Medal	
			" 6812 Pte A. ALLUM Military Medal.	
"	4		Training was carried out in accordance with attached programme	
"	5		The Battalion Training Staff paraded for Divine Service. No other parades were held today	

Army Form C. 2118.

WAR DIARY
or
INTELLIGENCE SUMMARY.
(Erase heading not required.)

Instructions regarding War Diaries and Intelligence Summaries are contained in F. S. Regs., Part II. and the Staff Manual respectively. Title pages will be prepared in manuscript.

Place	Date	Hour	Summary of Events and Information	Remarks and references to Appendices
REF. MAP:- HAZEBROUCK 5A VAUDRINGHEM	1918 May	6	Training was carried out in accordance with attached programme	
"	"	7	"	
"	"	8	"	
"	"	9	"	
"	"	10	2/Lieut G. BARRY reported today on completion of L.G. course at 1st Army School of Instruction	
"	"	11	Training was carried out in accordance with attached programme. 2/Lieut E.C. TURNER 11th Hants Regt reported for duty today and is attached to the Battalion Training Staff. 2/Lieut T.J. SHEFFIELD reported today on completion of course at 1st Army Scouting Observation and Sniping School. Capt C.J.D. LANKTREE and Capt. V.D. O'MALLEY M.C. proceeded on a course of instruction at 1st Army Infantry School.	
"	"	12	The Battalion Training Staff paraded for Divine Service. No other parade was held today.	

WAR DIARY
INTELLIGENCE SUMMARY

Army Form C. 2118.

Place	Date	Hour	Summary of Events and Information	Remarks and references to Appendices
Rgtl HQrs HAZEBROUCK 5th VAUDRINGHAM	May 13		In accordance with Battalion Operation Order No 1 the Battalion Training Staff marched to DIGNOPRÉ arriving in billets there at 3.15 p.m.	App.
			Under authority delegated by His Majesty the King, the Field Marshal Commanding in Chief has awarded the following decorations for gallantry in the Field :—	
			Lt Col H B TONSON-RYE — Distinguished Service Order	
			Capt (A/Major) B.H. PURDON — Military Cross	
			No 5499 R.S.M. J RING M.C.D.C.M. — Bar to Distinguished Conduct Medal.	
			Major H B TONSON-RYE is appointed Acting Lieut Col whilst commanding a Battalion. 5th April 1918. Auth. D.R.O. No 106/13/5/18.	
			Lieut W W Mc KEOWN is authorised to wear the badges of Rank of Captain under Auth D.R.O. No 102/12/5/18 and 16 Div ho A/501/33.	
Rgtl HQrs CALAIS DIGNOPRÉ	14		Training was carried out in accordance with attached programme	
	15		In accordance with Battalion Operation Order No 2 the Battalion Training Staff marched to DESVRES arriving in billets there at 4 p.m.	App.
DESVRES	16		Training was carried out in accordance with attached programme	

WAR DIARY
INTELLIGENCE SUMMARY
(Erase heading not required.)

Army Form C. 2118.

Place	Date	Hour	Summary of Events and Information	Remarks and references to Appendices
Rd Mt CALAIS DESVRES	May 17		Training was carried out in accordance with attached programme. Under authority delegated by the Field Marshal Commanding in Chief the VII Corps Cmdr has awarded the following decorations for acts of gallantry in the Field:- No 5758 Cpl J. WILLS. M.M. Bar to Military Medal. " 6852 Pte T. MacSWEENEY M.M. Bar to Military Medal " 7033 Sgt W. PAVER. Military Medal " 5571 Pte T. BENTLY. Military Medal	
	18		Training was carried out in accordance with attached programme.	
	19		In accordance with Battalion Operation Order No 3 the Battalion less Transport marched to HESDIN L'ABBE arriving in billets there at 9.15am. Training was carried out in accordance with attached programme.	
HESDIN L'ABBÉ	20		The Battalion 1st Line Transport with the exception of 1 Water Cart, 1 Mess Cart:1 Baggage Wagn and 7 Officers chargers was today handed over to the 2nd Bttn 59 Inf Regt of United States Army. The Transport and personnel proceeded to DESVRES at 6.30a.m. to report to Regimental Headquarters	

Army Form C. 2118.

WAR DIARY
or
INTELLIGENCE SUMMARY.
(Erase heading not required.)

Instructions regarding War Diaries and Intelligence Summaries are contained in F. S. Regs., Part II. and the Staff Manual respectively. Title pages will be prepared in manuscript.

Place	Date	Hour	Summary of Events and Information	Remarks and references to Appendices
Ref. No. CALAIS	1918			
HESDIN L'ABBÉ	May 20		59th American Infantry Brigade.	
"	" 21		Training was carried out in accordance with attached programme	
"	" 22		"	
"	" 23		"	
"	" 24		"	
"	" 25		"	
"	" 26		The Battalion Training Staff paraded for Divine Service. No other parades were held.	
"	" 27		Capt C.J.D. LANKTREE and Capt V.J. O'MALLEY M.C. departed for duty on completion of course of instruction at 1st Army Infantry School.	
"	" 28		58th Regt A.E.F. to which training staff is attached arrived today.	
"	" 29		Syndicates were attached for training, to battalions of 58th Regt.	
"	" 30		Training with American troops was continued today	
RACQUINGHEM	" 31	4.30 p.m.	Orders were received for the training Staff to proceed to the 31st Div. Arrived at RACQUINGHEM 7/Lt D.J. DAVIES posted to 7/8 Inniskilling's.	

2nd Battalion The Royal Mun Fusiliers.

TRAINING PROGRAMME FOR WEEK ENDING..... 4th May, 1918.

Date.	Time.	Place.	Nature of Exercise.	Remarks.
Monday 29th.	9.30.a.m.	Cross Roads 1/4 of miles S. of FLOYEC-QUES.	Lecture on Outposts.	C.Officer.
	10.30.a.m.	——DO——	A Picquet to be posted and all duties detailed.	Captn.C.C. Smythe. Picquet Commander.
	2.p.m.	VAUDRINGHEM.	Lectures on protection:- (a). At Rest. (b). When on the move.	C.Officer.
Tuesday. 30th.	9.a.m.	VAUDRINGHEM-FLOYECQUES-le-MESNIL.	Advanced and Rear Guards.	Captain. Lanktree.
	5.p.m.	VAUDRINGHEM School Room.	Lecture on Company in the Attack.	Major.B.H. Purdon.
WEDNES DAY. 1st May.	9.a.m.	VAUDRINGHEM.	Scheme for Company in Attack.	Major. Purdon, 2Lt. Barry.
	2.30.p.m.	——DO——	Lecture on Map Reading.	The C/O.
THURSDAY. 2nd May.	9.30.a.m.	Road Junction 1/4 mile S. of FLOYECQUES.	Map Reading.	The C.Offr.
	5.p.m.	VAUDRINGHEM School Room.	Lecture on Supply of Clothing and Rations in the Field.	Captain Lanktree.
FRIDAY. 3rd May.	9.a.m.	End of Road to N.of C.of FLOYEC-QUES.	Scheme for Fire Control and recognition of targets.	The C/O. Reg.S.Maj.
	5.p.m.	VAUDRINGHEM.	Lecture on Topography.	The C/O.
SATURDAY 4th May.	9.a.m.	VAUDRINGHEM.	Inter Communication and passing of Orders.	Captain. Smythe.
	2.p.m.	——DO——	Lecture on the Prismatic Compass.	The C/O.

In the Field. (sgd) H. TONSON-RYE. Lieutenant-Colonel.

27.4.18. Commanding 2nd Battalion The Royal Munster Fusiliers.

2nd Battalion The Royal Munster Fusiliers.

" TRAINING PROGRAMME FOR WEEK ENDING SATURDAY, 18TH MAY, 1918."

DATE.	TIME.	PLACE.	NATURE OF TRAINING.	REMARKS.
MAY, 1918 Monday, 13th.	9.to 10. a.m.	VAUDRINGHEM.	P. T. and B. F.	
	10.30.a.m.	FLOYECQUE S.	Scheme. Fire control & Recognition of targets.	
	2.p.m.	VAUDRINGHEM. -----DO-----	Drill. N.C.O's. Officer's Equitation class.	The R.S.M.)Compasses &)Maps to be)brought.
Tuesday, 14th.	9.to 10. a.m.	VAUDRINGHEM.	P. T. and B. F.	
	10.30.a.m.	FLOYECQUE-S Mill.	Coy in defence of a River crossing.	
	2.p.m.	VAUDRINGHEM.	Lecture by Divl Gas Officer.	)Dress:-)Fighting order)with Steel)Helmets.
Wednesday, 15th.	9.to 10. a.m.	VAUDRINGHEM.	P. T. and B. F.	
	10.30.a.m.	BRIOUVILL E.	Defence of a Village.	
	2.p.m.	VAUDRINGHEM.	Knotting & Lashing.	
Thursday, 16th.	9 to 10. a.m.	VAUDRINGHEM.	P. T. and B. F.	
	10.30.a.m.	DROUVILLE.	Company covering withdrawl of a Battalion.	
	3.p.m.	BLEQUIN RANGE.	)Musketry.	
Friday, 17th.	9.to 10. a.m.	VAUDRINGHEM.	P. T. and B. F.	
	10.30.a.m.	BOIS D THIEM- BRONNE.	)Formations for moving in woods,)Keeping touch, Changing direction,)etc.	
	2.p.m.	VAUDRINGHEM.	Drill. N.C.O's. Officer's Equitation class.	The R.S.M.
Saturday, 18th.	9.to 10. a.m.	VAUDRINGHEM.	P. T. and B. F.	
	10.30.a.m. to 11.a.m.	HORSE SHOW Fd.	Communication Drill.	The R.S.M.
	11.to 11. 30.a.m.	-----DO-----	)Fire positions and Rapid)loading and firing.	)Musketry)Instr
	11.30.a.m. to 12.30. p.m.	-----DO-----	)Handling of Arms.))	The R.S.M.
	3.p.m.	BLEQUIN RANGE.	Musketry.	

On Monday, Wednesday and Friday the Battalion Gas N.C.O. will instruct the Coy Gas N.C.O's, from 2.p.m. to 3.p.m.

xxxxxxxxxxxxxxxxxxxx xxxxxxxxxxxxxxxxxxxxxxxxxxxxxxxxxxxxxx

(Signed).H.B. TONSON-RYE, Lieutenant-Colonel,

Commanding 2nd Battalion The Royal Munster Fusiliers.

"2ND BATTALION THE ROYAL MUNSTER FUSILIERS."

TRAINING PROGRAMME OF ABOVE UNIT FOR WEEK ENDING :— 25/5/18.

DATE.	TIME.	PLACE.	NATURE OF TRAINING.	REMARKS.
May, 1918. Monday, 20th.	9.a.m.	HESDIN.	Lecture on United States Army Organisation & duties of Training Staff, etc.	
	10.a.m.) to 6.p.m.)	BILLETING AREA.	) Syndicates reconnoitering area.) Points:- Billets for Officer's) and men. Training grounds, etc.	
Tuesday, 21st.	9.a.m.	HESDIN.	As on Monday.	
	2.p.m.	---DO---	Drill.) C.Q.M.Sgts & Pioneers.) Cooking & construction of) Field Kitchens, etc.	Under the A/Qr.Master.
Wednesday, 22nd.	9.a.m.) 10.a.m.) 11.a.m.) 12 noon) 2.p.m.)	HESDIN	) P. T.) Bombing.)) Lecture on Lewis Gun.) Drill.) Gas instruction.	
Thursday, 23rd.	9.a.m.	On road to McAULL, 3 miles N.N.E.of HARDELOT Plage.	Route march. Protection on the move. Musketry.	
Friday, 24th.	9.a.m. 10.30.a.m 2.p.m.	HESDIN. LANDAC. HESDIN.	P. T. Protection at Rest. Musketry.) C.Q.M.Sgts & Pioneers,) Sanitation & Care of) Billets.	Under the A/Qr.Master.
Saturday, 25th.	9.a.m. 10.a.m. 11.a.m. 12 noon. 2.p.m.	HESDIN.	P. T. Bombing. Musketry. Drill. Gas Lecture.	

In the Field.   (signed). H.B.Touson-Rye. Lieut-Colonel.
19.5.18.   Commanding 2nd Battalion The Royal Munster Fusiliers.

2nd Bn the Royal Munster Fusiliers.

"TRAINING PROGRAMME FOR WEEK ENDING SATURDAY, 11TH MAY, 1918."

DATE.	TIME.	PLACE.	NATURE OF TRAINING.	REMARKS.
Monday. 6th May.	9.to 10.a.m.	VAUDRINGHEM.	P.T. and B.F.	
	10.30.a.m.	LE MESNIL.	Platoon in the attack. Flagged position to be reconnoitred & reported on by syndicates. Discussions on various points.	
	2.p.m.	VAUDRINGHEM.	Lecture on Engineering.	The C/O.
Tuesday, 7th May.	9.to 10.a.m.	----DO----	P.T. and B.F.	
	10.30.a.m.	2nd Class road running E.W. from LE MESNIL.	Platoon in the Defence. Method of taking up position, siting of trenches and working parties. Communications. Position of L.G. Mutual Support. Discussions on various points.	
	2.p.m.		HORSE SHOW.	
Wednesday, 8th May.	9.to 10.a.m.	VAUDRINGHEM.	P.T. and B.F.	
	10.30.a.m.	River Bridge ¾ mile E. of E.of/PLOYECQUES	Fire Orders & Fire positions.	
	11.a.m.		Compass March by day.	
	2.p.m.	VAUDRINGHEM.	Lecture. Night marching without a compass.	The C/O.
Thursday, 9th May.	9.to 10.a.m.	----DO----	P.T. and B.F.	
	10.30.a.m.	PLOYECQUES.	Scheme on Fire Control & recognition of targets.	
	3.p.m.	BLEQUIN RANGE.	Musketry.	
FRIDAY, 10th May.	9.to 10.a.m.	VAUDRINGHEM.	P.T. and B.F.	
	10.30.a.m.	LE MESNIL.	Company in attack. Formations. Mutual support. Communications. Consolidation. Discussions on various situations.	
	2.p.m.	VAUDRINGHEM.	Drill Demonstration.	R.S.M. J.Ring.
Saturday, 11th May.	9.to 10.a.m.	----DO----	P.T. and B.F.	
	10.30.a.m.		Company in the Defence. To embody the same points as on Tuesday.	
	3.p.m.	BLEQUIN RANGE.	Musketry.	

(Sgd) H.B. TONSON-RYE.

Lieut: Col:
Commdg: 2nd Bn. The Royal Munster Fusiliers.

Field.
5.5.18.

www.ingramcontent.com/pod-product-compliance
Lightning Source LLC
Chambersburg PA
CBHW081448160426
43193CB00013B/2406